THE LITTLE GUIDE TO

SHORELINES

THE LITTLE GUIDE TO
SHORELINES

Illustrations
by Tom Frost

Words by
Alison Davies

Hardie Grant

QUADRILLE

Introduction

Take a stroll along the shoreline and you enter a strange subliminal world, where land meets sea, a halfway paradise where the best of both realms convene. Whether you stand with your feet upon the sand, or dip a toe into the ocean, there is something magical about walking the line where the two connect. The creatures that exist here, the shells and flotsam washed up upon the beach, they all have something to add to the picture. They bring colour and curiosity, drama and vitality – they make the landscape bristle with life and, like the coastal backdrop, they are wonderfully unique.

From tiny shells and molluscs that battle to survive – and manage to thrive against the odds – to minute fish and colourful crabs, some blessed with the devil's bluster and those who take a more chilled approach to whatever comes their way, there is something for everyone; a different story in the making, it just depends on your preference.

If it's enchantment you crave, then you will find it in a whole host of creations that could have come from an artist's palette. They have been depicted so beautifully within these pages that you might wonder if they'll crawl out one day and make their way back to the shore. You'll find glorious anemones that sparkle like jewels in the midday sun and sensational sea stars, their curled rays extending outwards, as if beckoning you in. All manner of treasures teeter on the edge ready to plunge into the watery depths or find shelter deep within a rock face. You'll learn where to look for them, and how to identify each one. You'll also discover something of their narrative and what makes them so special.

This book invites you to take a walk through the pages and feel the sea breeze upon your skin. Enjoy the beauty of the shoreline, and let it reel you in.

'Hug the shore; let others try the deep.'

VIRGIL

Velvet Swimming Crab

Necora puber

FAMILY NAME Portunoidae

DESCRIPTION With bright red eyes, and back legs like paddles, this crab is usually brown or green in colour

SIZE Up to 9 cm (3½ in) along the carapace

HABITAT Beaches and rocky coastlines

DISTRIBUTION Found throughout European waters and coastlines

Also known as the Devil Crab because of its bright red eyes and feisty attitude, this eye-catching crustacean packs a powerful punch. Get too close and you might get a nasty nip, but if you were to pick one up you'd notice the soft velvety outer shell from which it gets its name. The velvet effect is thanks to a layer of fine hairs giving it a 'smooth to the touch' feel and appearance. An avid feeder on worms, sea snails and prawns, this crab is known for its bold character and enhanced swimming abilities. Its back legs work like paddles, propelling the crab through the water.

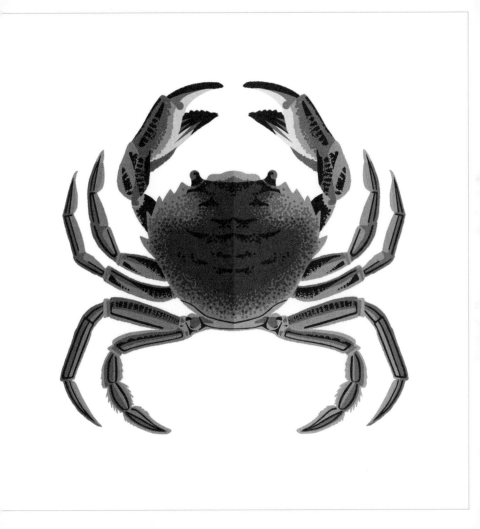

Royal Starfish

Astropecten articulatus

FAMILY NAME Astropectinidae

DESCRIPTION Has five arms that are purple in hue, as is the central disc;
it's outlined with an orange margin

SIZE Its arms can grow to between 2 and 8 cm (¾ and 3⅛ in) in length

HABITAT Found on sandy bottoms at depths of up to 165 m (541 ft)

DISTRIBUTION Found in the western Atlantic including the east coast
of the United States, the Gulf of Mexico and the Caribbean Sea

This gorgeous starfish has a tendency to overeat, which can
prove fatal if it ruptures its central disc. That said, when it
does snack it has five sets of jaws that it uses to swallow its
prey whole. Clams are the meal of choice, but it's unable
to digest the shell so this is regurgitated. With only one
opening, this starfish uses its mouth to eat and excrete
waste. The beautiful purple hue is the reason for its name,
as this is the colour most often associated with monarchs.

Tidepool Sculpin

Oligocottus maculosus

FAMILY NAME Cottidae

DESCRIPTION A small fish with a tapering body and dorsal and anal fins; it has darker blotches on its back

SIZE Grows up to 8 cm (3⅛ in) in length

HABITAT Found in sheltered spots, and temperate water, in tidepools

DISTRIBUTION Found in the north Pacific Ocean, from the Sea of Okhotsk and Bering Sea down towards the west coast of the United States

This mottled mercurial fish has five irregular splodges known as 'saddles' upon its back. As its name might suggest, it's commonly found under rocks and in tidepools along the shoreline. Usually found at depths no more than 9 m (29½ ft), this tiny fish can tolerate both high and low salinities, so even when it's trapped in a tidepool it can survive. Although it's usually a grey-green in hue, it can change colour to blend in with its surroundings, making it easier to ensnare prey. Its favourite eats include small invertebrates, isopods, amphipods, shrimps and worms. The Tidepool Sculpin has a lifespan of five years.

Common Nutmeg

Cancellaria reticulata

FAMILY NAME Cancellariidae

DESCRIPTION A small, sculpted shell with ridges, and six or seven whorls; usually a pale yellowish or cream hue, with orangey-brown bands

SIZE Grows up to around 4.8 cm (1⅞ in)

HABITAT Lives in offshore waters, the shell is often found washed up on beaches

DISTRIBUTION Found in the western Atlantic, the Caribbean Sea, the Gulf of Mexico and the Lesser Antilles

This medium-sized mollusc lives on warm sandy shores. Its handsome shell is a popular beach find and prized for the pattern of rust brown bands that decorate the outer surface. The Common Nutmeg is named because it resembles the seed of the Nutmeg plant, while the family name evolves from the word cancellate meaning 'lattice-like'. This relates to the ribs and spirals that seem to interlace and cross each other on the outer surface.

Hermit Crab

Paguroidea

FAMILY NAME Coenobitidae

DESCRIPTION Reddish brown in colour, the Hermit Crab borrows its shell from sea snails; its right hand pincer is longer than its left

SIZE Length of the body is around 3.5 cm (1⅜ in)

HABITAT Rocky shorelines, commonly found in rock pools

DISTRIBUTION Most common in the cooler waters of Northern Europe

There are over 800 types of Hermit Crab throughout the world. Most of these live in the ocean, although some are land-dwellers. Unlike other crabs they cannot grow their own shell so they 'borrow' their home from sea snails or whelks. Their body has a curled tail with a hook, which allows them to slot neatly inside. Once they've found a shell to coil up in they must be prepared to fight for it, as other Hermit Crabs will try to evict them. This usually takes the form of a challenge in which the contender knocks on the shell to draw the existing crab out so battle can commence. The victor wins a new home, while the loser is left in the cold.

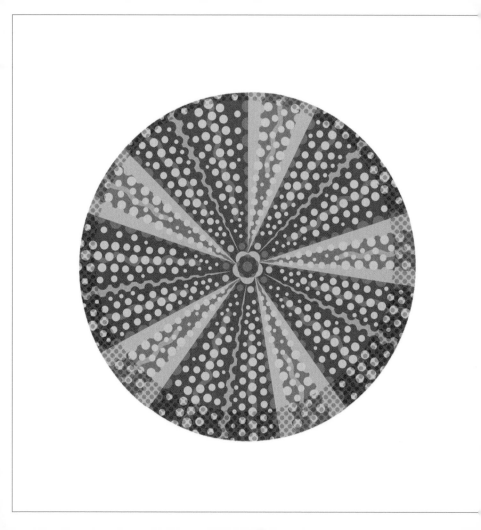

Common Sea Urchin

Echinus esculentus

FAMILY NAME Echinidae

DESCRIPTION A large globular urchin, with short, sturdy spines; usually a pinkish purple shade, although it can be red, green or yellow

SIZE Grows up to 15 cm (6 in) in diameter

HABITAT Found on the seabed at depths of up to 40 m (131 ft), and sometimes in rock pools

DISTRIBUTION Found in the northeast Atlantic, from Iceland to Finland and Norway, and also south to Portugal; also common on British shores

The steady Common Sea Urchin is a slow moving grazer. It likes to feed on seaweeds, bryrozoans and barnacles, but will snack on anything within its hungry grasp. While it may take its time it's hard to ignore, having short spines and a stunning rosy hue. Its scientific name *Echinus* comes from the Greek word for 'hedgehog' and it's easy to see where this comparison came from. Prized as an edible delicacy, the Common Sea Urchin was more than just a food source to the ancients. In Nordic countries, the fossils were treasured and believed to be thunderbolts from the Norse god Thor.

Conch Shells

FAMILY NAME Strombidae

DESCRIPTION Spiral conical shells, often brightly coloured, with a twisted spire at one end

SIZE Vary in size, but Queen Conches can grow up to 30 cm (11¾ in) in length

HABITAT Shallow sandy beaches, on tropical reefs and in seagrass beds

DISTRIBUTION In tropical waters throughout the world, including the Caribbean, West Indies and Mediterranean

The conch is a marine snail, with a shell that is much sought after by collectors. Triangular in shape and often ornate, the shell of the Queen Conch is much larger than others, with a vibrant pink inner surface. Conch produce hundreds of thousands of eggs, but only a few develop into adults. It usually takes four years for the snail to grow its shell and reach full maturity. In Buddhism, the shell is one of the eight auspicious symbols known as the Ashtamangala, and is associated with the gentle melody of the Buddha's voice. To the Hindus the conch was an essential tool of the God Vishnu, and an emblem of power and authority.

Black Tegula

Tegula funebralis

FAMILY NAME Tegulidae

DESCRIPTION This medium-sized snail has a thick dark purple to black shell, with a whorled cone

SIZE Grows up to 3 cm (1¼ in) diameter

HABITAT Found on open, exposed coastlines under rocky outcrops

DISTRIBUTION Found along the Pacific coast of North America to Baja California

Also known as the Black Turban Snail, because of the rounded cone shape of its shell that resembles a turban, this fascinating creature has a lifespan of between 80 and 100 years. It's no surprise then that it has mastered the art of escaping predators. If attacked on a slope, it will detach its foot so that it can roll away. Sometimes it will climb on top of its predator's shell to avoid capture. The foot, which can be seen poking from the aperture, varies in shade depending on the sex of the snail, and males have a paler foot bottom than females. Discarded Tegula shells are often commandeered by the Hermit Crab (see page 16).

Gooseneck Barnacle

Pollicipes polymerus

FAMILY NAME Pollicipedidae

DESCRIPTION These barnacles have a long fleshy stem that protrudes from a white shell, where the creature lives

SIZE The body grows up to 4.5 cm (1¾ in), while the stalk can reach 15 cm (6 in) in length

HABITAT Clamped to rock faces, they're continually battered by the sea

DISTRIBUTION Found from southeast Alaska to Baja California

To food connoisseurs the Gooseneck Barnacle is a rare delicacy that finds its place on only the most exclusive menus. This unusual looking crustacean has a long neck, which to medieval naturalists resembled a goose neck, hence the name. As they were unable to observe the faraway breeding grounds of some species of geese, they came to the strange conclusion that these weirdly shaped barnacles were in fact goslings fallen from their rocky perches into the sea. Living in large colonies attached to the rock face, the Gooseneck Barnacle is a sedentary creature and a filter feeder that relies on water movement to eat.

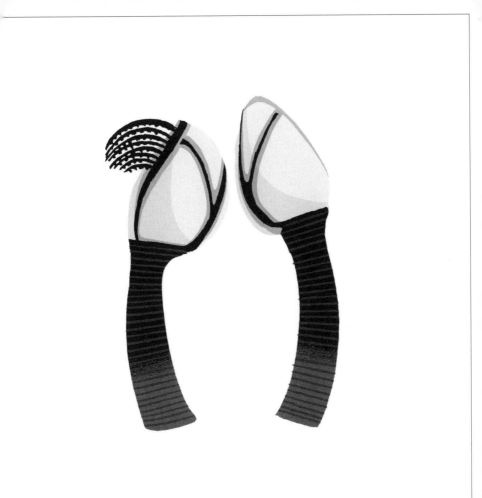

Mermaid's Purse

DESCRIPTION A black or brown leathery looking pouch with
tendrils or horns at each end

SIZE Varies, anything from 5–12 cm (2–4¾ in) in length

HABITAT Washed up on beaches, or tangled in seaweed

DISTRIBUTION Found anywhere in the world

A Mermaid's Purse is a leathery pouch used to house
the fertilised egg of a shark or ray. This neatly fashioned
case is a detachable uterus, which is secreted somewhere
on the seabed, often submerged in a seagrass meadow
or in a rock crevice. Made out of fibrous protein
collagen, it's super durable and protects the growing
embryo inside. The case detaches from the seabed as the
shark or ray hatches, which means that found ones are
usually empty. Long, slender Purses with tendrils tend to
belong to the Spotted Catshark, while squatter, square
shaped ones with horns in each corner come from rays.

Whelk Shells

FAMILY NAME Buccinidae

DESCRIPTION A conical shell with a wavy, fold-like pattern on the surface

SIZE Can grow up to 10 cm (4 in) in length

HABITAT Sandy seabeds and shores, often found in shallow tide pools

DISTRIBUTION From Iceland and Norway down to the Bay of Biscay and throughout the north Atlantic

This striking spiralled shell is hard to miss upon the seashore. The whorls that form the outer casing are produced by the creature's mantle, which emits a calcium carbonate that stretches around the central axis as the shell grows. It's an impressive feat of natural architecture, and it's not just prized by humans. The Hermit Crab (see page 16) is also a fan, and will grab a discarded shell to make its home. The colour of the shell varies depending on which part of the world it hails from, but the most common shade is pale brown with a pink interior.

Serrated Wrack

Fucus serratus

FAMILY NAME Fucaceae

DESCRIPTION Olive brown, and shrubby, with strap-like fronds
that have jagged, serrated edges

SIZE The plant grows to around 60 cm (23⅜ in) in length

HABITAT Found on rocky and sheltered coastlines

DISTRIBUTION Found around the coastline of the British Isles,
and throughout the north Atlantic

Also known as Toothed Wrack and Saw Wrack because of
the sharp edged fronds, this dense seaweed grows just above
the low water mark. The female of the species releases
more than a million eggs, which emit a pheromone that's
irresistible to the sperm, which is why this seaweed is in
abundance. Home to a number of different gasteropods,
including flat Periwinkles, Serrated Wrack is the ideal hiding
place, providing shelter and shade in and around rock pools.
Other seaweeds such as Dulse also grow amongst the fronds.

Common Mussel

Mytilus edulis

FAMILY NAME Mytilidae

DESCRIPTION Triangular in shape, the shell is usually a greyish blue, although they can also be brown, and features concentric lines

SIZE Usually ranges between 5–10 cm (2–4 in), although they can reach up to 20 cm (7⅞ in)

HABITAT Rocky coasts, sandy, muddy, and open shorelines, in crevices and on piers

DISTRIBUTION Common around the world, except the polar regions

The Common Mussel, which is also known as the Blue Mussel, is a bivalve, which means it has two shells that clamp together. A popular choice on most seafood menus, it's also favoured by Oystercatchers, Starfish, Crabs and Dog Whelks. Forming large and dense mussel beds, which are anchored to the seabed by byssal threads, mussels eat by filtering detritus from the water. The sticky tuft of threads that keeps each one in place is also known as a 'beard'. Being super strong, these threads are able to withstand the harshest seas.

Woolly Sculpin

Clinocottus analis

FAMILY NAME Cottidae

DESCRIPTION This fish can be green, greenish black and also slightly reddish in tint; it has a mottled, elongated body, and a large, flattened head

SIZE Up to 18 cm (7 in) in length

HABITAT Lives in the seabed, and is commonly found in tidepools

DISTRIBUTION Found in the Mexican waters of the Pacific Ocean; also found from just south of Guerrero Negro and northward along the central and northwest coasts of Baja California

The Woolly Sculpin, known as the *Charrasco Lanudo* in Spanish, lives in waters up to 18 m (26 ft) deep. Like the Tidepool Sculpin (see page 12) it can adapt to its environment and change colour to fit in; ideal for sourcing its next meal. It feasts mainly upon crustaceans, fish eggs, larvae and molluscs; most of its diet is translucent making it easy to spot amongst dark algae. Able to breathe air, the Woolly Sculpin can survive for 24 hours out of water. The male has a lifespan of up to eight years, the female up to six years.

Common Limpet

Patella vulgata

FAMILY NAME Patellidae

DESCRIPTION A cone-shaped shell, with radiating ridges and growth lines; the shell is usually greyish white, although it can have a yellow tint

SIZE Up to 6 cm (2⅜ in) in length

HABITAT Rocky shorelines and rock pools

DISTRIBUTION Found from Norway to the Mediterranean

The Common Limpet is a type of snail, and the superhero of the mollusc kingdom. While it appears to be little more than a small conical shell usually seen stuck to the side of rock pools, there's more to this creature than meets the eye. When the tide comes in the Common Limpet truly shines. It scales the surface of its rocky home in a gradual movement, feeding off the algae with its impressive tongue – the world's strongest known biological structure. When the tide goes out it returns to its favourite spot by tracing the path of mucus left behind. This spot becomes home when the edges dry out to form a scar; the limpet uses this to fix itself firmly in place.

Quartz Veins

DESCRIPTION Thin vein-like strands of quartz, which come in a range of hues and run through the basalt rocks

SIZE Varies in size and shape

HABITAT Seen cutting through lumps of rock on the beach

DISTRIBUTION Rocky coasts and shorelines around the world

While Quartz Veins may appear like threads running through the seams of a rock, the reality is that they're more like thin sheets of quartz that have formed over time. Most often they appear gradually to fill an already present crack within the rock. Quartz Veins are usually milky white in appearance, but they gradually become clear as crystal growth slows. While the veins might not necessarily develop into quartz crystals, if you follow a thread it may lead you to a natural fissure where you could find an embedded crystal.

Baltic Tellin

Limecola balthica

FAMILY NAME Tellinidae

DESCRIPTION A circular, slightly tapered shell defined by umbones; it comes in a range of shades and is either evenly coloured or has concentric bands

SIZE Small, up to 2.5 cm (1 in) in length

HABITAT Found on tidal flats and near estuaries, usually just beneath the sand or mud

DISTRIBUTION Common around the British Isles and found in the coastal waters of the north Atlantic and north Pacific Oceans

This small saltwater clam is a marine mollusc that is commonly found on beaches near estuaries. Its beautifully moulded round shell, often with concentric lines, comes in a range of hues, from white and pink to orange, red, yellow, purple and blue. The variation of colour comes from sulphates within the sediment and also as a result of predation by sea birds. A stunning jewel of the beach and a popular find for shell-seekers, the Baltic Tellin is infaunal, meaning that it can be found buried just under the surface of the sand.

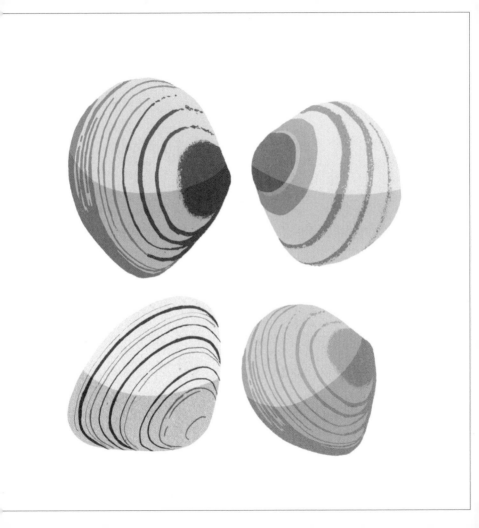

Shore Crab

Carcinus maenas

FAMILY NAME Portunidae

DESCRIPTION With a pentagon shaped and serrated shell, this crab is mostly green, but can also be red or yellow

SIZE Up to 10 cm (4 in) in length

HABITAT Sandy beaches, rocky coasts, salt marshes and in other vegetation

DISTRIBUTION Most common in Europe and North Africa

This hardy little character is incredibly resilient and can survive out of water for five days or more. Also known as the European Green Crab, it is invasive and upsets the balance of marine ecosystems because it feeds on a wide variety of animals, including other crabs, oysters, clams and juvenile lobsters. It also destroys shellfish beds. With a life span of between four and seven years, the female of the species releases around 185,000 eggs, sometimes twice a year. Highly territorial, this crustacean has three blunt spines between the eyes, and five pointed spines on either side. Usually olive green, youngsters start life a light sandy shade.

Irish Moss or Carrageen

Chondrus crispus

FAMILY NAME Gigartinaceae

DESCRIPTION Irish Moss comes in a range of colours, from greenish yellow to red and dark purple; it's a thin seaweed, with blade-like fronds that fan outwards

SIZE Fronds vary from 5–25 cm (2–9⅞ in) in length

HABITAT Grows on rocky coastlines

DISTRIBUTION Can be found along the Atlantic coast of the British Isles, continental Europe and North America

Despite its name, Irish Moss, sometimes known as Carrageen, is a species of red algae made of a jelly-like substance called carrageenan, which can be extracted by boiling the fronds. This ingredient is used as a gelatin substitute in vegan foods, and as a general emulsifier. It's harvested by dredging shallow waters or picking up discarded fronds on beaches. If eaten, it's thought to protect the gut by promoting good bacteria and it's also high in fibre. The 'Irish' connection in the name stems from its popularity during the potato famine in Ireland in the 1800s, when it was eaten as a substitute.

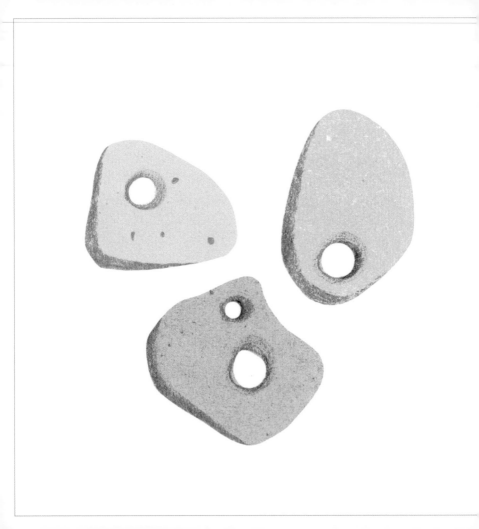

Hag Stones

DESCRIPTION Vary in size, shape and colour, but the one thing they all have in common is a hole through the stone

SIZE Can be any size, but are usually small to medium

HABITAT Dry riverbeds, coastal shorelines

DISTRIBUTION Anywhere in the world where you might find a beach or shoreline

Also known as Adder Stones, Fairy Stones and Holy Stones, these gifts of the shoreline feature in folklore from around the world. The hole at the centre is what makes them special. This occurs naturally over time when stones and pebbles rub together, but it also happens when a bivalve known as a Piddock bores into the centre of the stone. The name Hag Stone comes from Europe. The ancients believed the curious appearance of these stones gave them magical powers. They were worn as protective amulets and hung above barn doors, windows and in boats, to keep evil at bay. A powerful talisman, the Hag Stone is thought to prevent witchcraft, and if you dare look through the hole you might even glimpse other worlds and spirits.

Cowrie Shells

Cypraea

FAMILY NAME Cypraeidae

DESCRIPTION A beautiful glossy or speckled shell, thick in consistency and almost egg shaped; the apertural lips that open into the first whirl are often finely toothed

SIZE Vary in size, but some like the Golden Cowrie can reach up to 11 cm (4⅜ in) in length

HABITAT On coastlines and rocky shores

DISTRIBUTION Found in the coastal waters of the Indian and Pacific Oceans

This eye-catching shell has a long history of being used as a form of currency in cultures from West Africa to China and India. No wonder when you catch a glimpse of its shiny, shimmering surface. Cowries were also used to decorate clothes and masks, and West African warriors wore them when going into battle as a symbol of protection. Their link to the ocean meant they were blessed by the Goddess Yemaya and had the potential to keep evil at bay. Some Native American tribes were also fans, believing them to be highly sacred and using them in rituals for spiritual growth and healing.

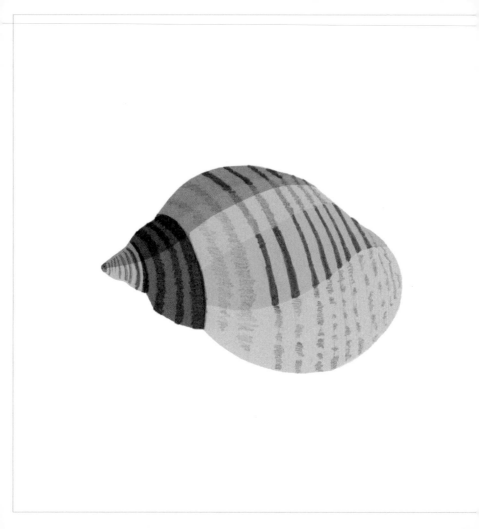

Dog Whelk

Nucella lapillus

FAMILY NAME Muricidae

DESCRIPTION A broadly conical shell, with a pointed spire and ridges; usually white, grey or brown in hue

SIZE Usually up to 3 cm (1¼ in) in length, although some grow to 6 cm (2⅜ in)

HABITAT Rocky shores, from the mid shore downwards

DISTRIBUTION Around the coasts of Europe, the northwest Atlantic coast of America and Atlantic coasts

This predatory sea snail feeds on mussels and barnacles, but this is no simple task! The Dog Whelk bores through the shell of its victim and injects it with an enzyme. The result is a liquified soup, which the whelk sucks from the outer casing; a practice that can take several days. Once the whelk is satisfied it retires to a crevice to rest. While this might sound macabre, the Dog Whelk needs to be careful. Should it stumble onto a dense mussel bed it can become trapped by the sticky byssal threads and starve to death. The animal within the pointed shell is rarely seen and is usually a white or cream colour.

Bladderwrack

Fucus vesiculosus

FAMILY NAME Fucaceae

DESCRIPTION Brownish green in shade, with branching fronds and air
filled pockets known as 'bladders'

SIZE Up to 90 cm (35½ in) in length

HABITAT Grows between high and low water marks on rocky shorelines

DISTRIBUTION Widely distributed in the north Atlantic

A common sight on beaches around the world, Bladderwrack, also
known as Black Tang and Rockweed, is a type of seaweed that resembles
bubble wrap. The bladders, which run along the length of the plant, are
air-filled pockets that allow it to float upright when in the water. Once
submerged this seaweed absorbs the nutrients it needs to flourish. Often
growing in dense beds along with other types of seaweed, Bladderwrack
provides shelter and nourishment for a variety of marine life, including
the Periwinkle. The Romans were fans and used it in preparations
for aching joints, while in folk magic it was a common ingredient in
protection spells, especially for those travelling over water.

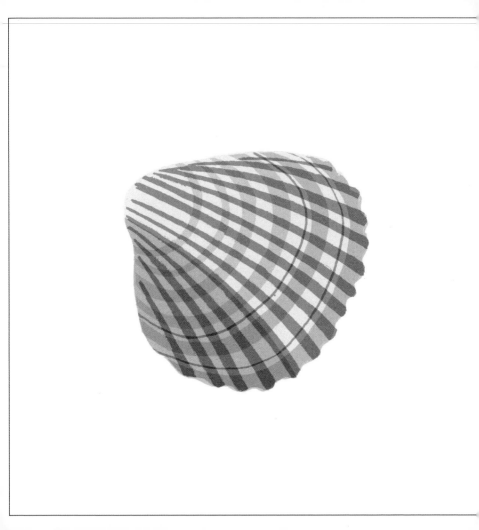

Common Cockle

Cerastoderma edule

FAMILY NAME Cardiidae

DESCRIPTION The shell is broad, oval in shape and thick, with 22–28 radiating ribs; the outer is off white or yellowy brown, the inside dull white sometimes purple-tinged

SIZE Up to 5 cm (2 in) in length

HABITAT Can live in most types of sand, usually found in estuaries or sheltered bays

DISTRIBUTION Widely distributed, from the Barents Sea to the Iberian peninsular, and also along the coast of West Africa

The Common Cockle, like its name suggests, is a popular shoreline feature and a tasty snack favoured by humans and shore birds alike. With its round clam-like shell it's easy to spot and can be found on most sandy beaches – it survives by filtering plankton and other organic matter from the water. While Common Cockles are abundant and can reach a density of 10,000 per square meter (10¾ square feet), they don't tend to grow in winter. This results in the growth lines clearly seen on the shell, which help to identify its age. As they live in the top few layers of sediment, cockle beds are often destroyed in strong storms.

Blood Star

Henricia leviuscula

FAMILY NAME Echinasteridae

DESCRIPTION Bright orange to russet red in hue with a central disc that has patches of grey, this star has five thin arms

SIZE Grows up to 12 cm (4¾ in) in diameter

HABITAT Lives in rock pools, crevices and caves

DISTRIBUTION Found on the west coast of North America, from Alaska to California and Mexico; also found in the eastern Pacific Ocean on the coasts of Siberia and Japan

This vibrant star may be one of the smallest in the sea, but what it lacks in size it makes up for in eye-catching splendour. The vivid burnt orange shade eventually fades when the creature dies, a fact that many collectors miss when they retrieve them from the beach. Like other sea stars, it can regenerate an arm even though it doesn't have a brain. The Blood Star feeds on plankton sponges, and small bacteria, which it coats in mucus and draws into its mouth.

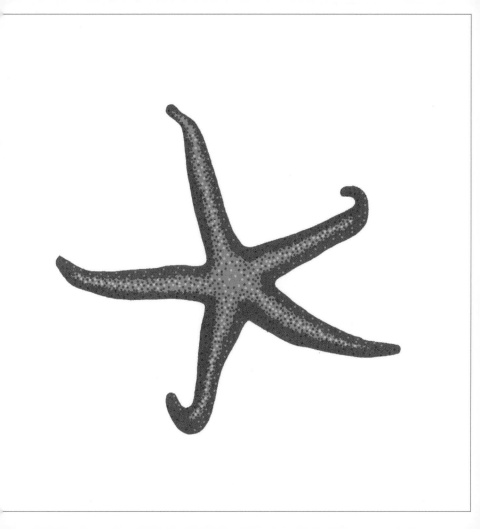

Granite Pebbles

DESCRIPTION Shaped like an egg, with a smooth granite grey appearance
SIZE This varies, although you can usually fit them into the palm of your hand
HABITAT Found on rocky and pebble beaches
DISTRIBUTION Worldwide

Most beach pebbles are igneous and metamorphic stones made of granite. They form when molten rock from magma and lava eventually cools down. Over time the stones take shape and, like all others on the beach, become more polished and defined by the wear and tear of footfall and the weathering process of the sea. These ovoid pebbles are prized for their appearance and are often used as paperweights and table decorations.

Sea Lettuce

Ulva lactuca

FAMILY NAME Ulvaceae

DESCRIPTION Sea lettuce is bright green, and has ruffled fronds that resemble lettuce leaves

SIZE Length up to 20 cm (7⅞ in), frond width around 30 cm (11¾ in)

HABITAT Rocky coastlines, often found clinging to the sides of rock pools

DISTRIBUTION Found throughout the world, including Europe, North and Central America, southwest Asia, Australia, New Zealand and the Caribbean Islands

Like its leafy vegetable namesake, at its freshest Sea Lettuce is a vibrant, translucent green. It has floppy fronds that are remarkably strong and grip rocks and boulders. It tends to flourish in nutrient-rich waters, and should it become detached from its original rocky holdfast it forms large floating colonies. Often used in cooking – in soups, stews, and salads – it's also used as 'green laver', an ingredient in Welsh laver bread. If you fancy cooking up a storm with this nutritious weed, harvest from spring to mid-summer.

Common Starfish

Asterias rubens

FAMILY NAME Asteriidae

DESCRIPTION Has five arms and is covered in small spines;
it's orange in hue

SIZE Diameter of 10–30 cm (4–11¾ in)

HABITAT Rocky coasts and out at sea, most often found in rock
pools and washed up on the shore

DISTRIBUTION Found throughout the northeast Atlantic region

Despite being 'nose-less', the Common Starfish has a keen sense of
smell thanks to an array of receptors within the skin. This ability to
pick up scent draws them in huge swathes to mussel and oyster beds,
as well as other food sources. To eat their prey they prize open the
shell with their arms and insert their stomach inside. Their impressive
digestive juices get to work dissolving their shellfish dinner, after which
they reabsorb the full stomach. They also have the ability to regenerate
limbs – a nifty trick that means there's no need to worry if they shed
an arm fleeing a predator. It will always grow back, given time!

Auger Shell

Turritellinella tricarinata

FAMILY NAME Turritellidae

DESCRIPTION A slender, sharply pointed cone, with up to 20 whorls containing ridges; usually off-white, pale pink and brown in tone

SIZE Grows up to 3 cm (1¼ in) in length and 1 cm (⅜ in) wide

HABITAT Usually found deep under water; also found in muddy pools of shallow water

DISTRIBUTION Common in the Mediterranean, from Norway to North Africa

Also known as the Great Screw Shell or the Common Turret Snail, this predatory gastropod sits on the seabed, where it filters particles of food from the seawater. It may be slow moving but don't be fooled: it uses its radular tool to inject venom and capture worms. The clever Auger remains buried, making it hard to see at first glance, but it still maintains contact with the water. For this reason it's often associated with the element of water and is considered a tool to promote intuition in mystical circles. In ancient cultures, from China to Egypt, the shell was prized and seen as an emblem of peace. Used in shamanic rituals, the Auger was also carried as a protective talisman.

Oarweed

Laminaria digitata

FAMILY NAME Laminariaceae

DESCRIPTION A kelp seaweed with fronds split
into long ribbons, darkish brown to green in colour

SIZE Up to 2 m (6½ ft) in length

HABITAT Rocky coasts and seabeds

DISTRIBUTION Grows in the north Atlantic and
Arctic Oceans and in and around the North Sea

This hardy seaweed is usually found in shallow seas, where the
sunlight reaches the ocean bed, and it's a common sight on craggy
coastlines. Its roots form strong holdfasts that anchor it in place, and
also provide the perfect sanctuary for all manner of sea creatures,
including worms and sea spiders. Also known as Tangleweed and Sea
Ribbon, the finger-like fronds can resemble hands from a distance as
they cling to the rocks. Oarweed has been a food source for humans
for thousands of years, most likely because it is plentiful and easy
to find. It is rich in amino acids, and is also used as fertiliser.

Mediterranean Green Crab

Carcinus aestuarii

FAMILY NAME Carcinidae
DESCRIPTION Very similar to the Shore Crab (see page 43) in hue and appearance
SIZE Up to 6 cm (2⅜ in) in length
HABITAT Rocky shores and reefs, salt marshes
DISTRIBUTION Mediterranean Sea, Black Sea and the Sea of Azov

At one time this was considered a subspecies of the Shore Crab because of their similarity in size and colour, but studies have shown that it is a species in its own right. The carapace of the Shore is short and toothed; in the Mediterranean the space between the eyes is longer and smoother. Also the gonopods, or genital appendages, are straight, while those of the Shore are curved. This crab feeds on small crustacean, bivalves, algae and dead marine life, but it adapts its diet depending on the season and its habitat.

Sea Glass

DESCRIPTION Colourful glass with a frosted appearance

SIZE Can be any size, depending on the origin, but tends to have round smooth edges

HABITAT Sandy beaches alongside salt water

DISTRIBUTION It is found all over the world, but beaches in Mexico, Hawaii, Italy, Spain and Scotland are famous for an abundance of sea glass

Sea Glass is formed from broken and discarded glass bottles and pottery, which have been tumbled in the ocean for many years to give a distinctively frosted appearance. Any sharp edges have been smoothed by the waves to reveal gleaming jewels in an array of colours. The shade depends on the original hue of the glass. The most common colours are green, brown, white and clear. Also known as Mermaid's Tears, legend has it that when a mermaid fell for a sailor, Neptune – the Greek god of the ocean – would banish her to the seabed. Here she would weep for many days, and her tears would rise to surface to become twinkling jewels and tokens of her love.

Sand Dollars

Dendraster excentricus

FAMILY NAME Clypeasteroida

DESCRIPTION Rounded in shape, these urchins have a flattened body and tiny spines that feel like brushed velvet when touched

SIZE Vary in size from 5–15 cm (2–6 in) in diameter

HABITAT They live below the tideline in sand and sandy mud bottoms

DISTRIBUTION Found in the Northern Hemisphere in temperate and tropical waters

Also known as Sea Cookies and Snapper Biscuits, Sand Dollars are a type of sea urchin renowned for their token-like shape. Their rigid outer skeleton, called a 'test', is made up of five symmetrical calcium bicarbonate plates, which remain complete after the creature dies. They're a top find of beachcombers, who consider them a lucky omen. In folklore the Sand Dollar is a symbol of peace, and the five symmetrical slits in the test are often linked to the five wounds of Christ on the cross. More recently, scientists have discovered that some Sand Dollars can clone themselves.

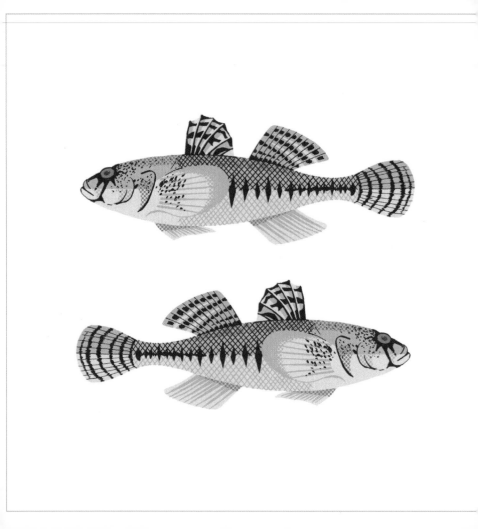

Common Goby

Pomatoschistus microps

FAMILY NAME Gobiidae

DESCRIPTION A tiny fish, sandy in colour; it has a pair of dorsal fins and a pelvic fin that fuses into a suction cup

SIZE Grows up to 6.4 cm (2½ in) in length

HABITAT Shallow sandy pools and estuaries

DISTRIBUTION Along British coastlines and also found further south towards Portugal and north to Norway

This scaleless fish is a bottom dweller, living and feeding low in the water. It is notoriously hard to spot, as it blends in with its environment thanks to the sandy hue of its body. While it may not be as brightly coloured as some of its European cousins, it is a master of disguise – which is just as well for it only has a short life span of up to 15 months. During this time the female will lay her eggs beneath a shell, leaving the male to keep watch for around two weeks until the eggs hatch. The male displays a dark blotch at the rear of its dorsal fin during the breeding season, making it easier to distinguish between the two.

Purple Shore Crab

Hemigrapsus nudus

FAMILY NAME Varunidae

DESCRIPTION Adults are commonly purple, but they can also range from yellow to green and reddish brown; their claws have reddish spots and white tips

SIZE 4–5.6 cm (1½–2¼ in) across the carapace

HABITAT Usually found in shallow waters and along rocky coastlines

DISTRIBUTION Found along the west coast of North America, from Alaska to Baja California

These diminutive crabs may be small, but what they lack in size they make up for in adaptability. They can regulate the amount of salt in their bodies, which means they can live in saltmarshes and other brackish terrains. With a square carapace, and legs that usually match their purple hue, they lack the fine bristles common in other crabs – because of this they're also known as Naked Shore Crabs. Slow and steady wins the race when it comes to growth, and this crab takes a full three years to reach maturity. When mating, males and females perform a strange dance that sees them embrace, belly to belly.

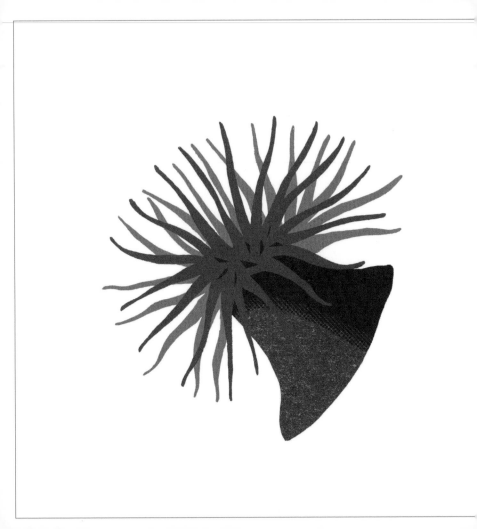

Beadlet Anemone

Actinia equina

FAMILY NAME Actiniidae

DESCRIPTION Squat and stocky in appearance, with stubby thick tentacles; is usually a deep blood red but can also be green or orange in tone

SIZE Around 5 cm (2 in) in diameter

HABITAT Rocky shores and coastlines, in rock pools

DISTRIBUTION Throughout Western Europe, the Mediterranean and from the Arctic to the west coast of Africa

This treasure of the sea may look like a ruby red jewel lurking at the bottom of a rock pool, but don't be fooled – when the tide goes out it retracts its tentacles, leaving only a blob of brightness that belies its true nature. When the tide comes in the beautiful Beadlet Anemone will reveal its tentacles once more. It is highly territorial and fiercely protects its patch from intruders by unleashing the stinging power of its blue beads, which are found beneath the tentacles. It also uses these to secure a meal, by stinging passing prey such as small fish and crabs.

Pink Sea Star

Pisaster brevispinus

FAMILY NAME Asteriidae

DESCRIPTION Pink to lavender in colour, this star has five arms
that extend from a central disc

SIZE Can grow between 51–71 cm (20–28 in) in diameter

HABITAT Usually seen in muddy or sandy subtidal areas, often on
floats and pilings

DISTRIBUTION Found along the Pacific Coast of North America,
from Alaska to southern California

The stunning colour of this creature is the first thing to catch the
eye, along with its size. It is one of the largest sea stars in the world,
and is also known as the Giant Pink Sea Star or the Short Spined
Sea Star because of its smooth texture. A scavenger when it comes
to sourcing food, it will often feast on dead fish and other animals.
It does this by extending its stomach over its prey to digest it. Like
many other sea stars it's able to regenerate a limb if the central disc
remains intact, but it will swiftly dry out when exposed to air.

Sea Hare

Aplysia punctata

FAMILY NAME Aplysiidae

DESCRIPTION Similar to a sea slug in appearance, but the
upper head has tentacles that resemble a hare's ears; usually
a rosy mauve colour, they can also be greenish-blue

SIZE 7–20 cm (2¾–7⅞ in) in length

HABITAT Sheltered, coastal waters in amongst thick vegetation

DISTRIBUTION Around the British Isles

This fascinating marine snail gets its name from the long rhinophores
on its head, but while they might look like ears they are in fact used
for tasting particles in the water. Avid seaweed grazers, their unique
colour comes from their favourite snack – those with a preference for
green algae are usually greenish-blue in colour, while those that favour
red algae have the typical rosy hue. These striking gastropods don't
carry a shell; instead they keep a tiny transparent shell internally.
Despite their unusual appearance they're not ones to draw attention,
and prefer slow moving waters where they can hide in patches of sand.

Scallop Shells

FAMILY NAME Pectinidae

DESCRIPTION Two fan-shaped shells, which are symmetrical and connected by a hinge

SIZE Range in size from 2.5–15 cm (1–6 in) in width

HABITAT As scallops must live in saltwater, the shells are often found discarded on beaches, shorelines and rocky coasts

DISTRIBUTION Can be found in oceans all over the world

A beachcomber's delight, these shells are prized for the beauty of their symmetrical fan shape and colour. Each shell has an array of 'eyes' dotted around the rim, but rather than improve the mollusc's eyesight they act as a warning to hopeful predators. Notoriously fast movers, scallops can speed through water so their shell is much thinner than their plodding counterparts who need the protection of a thicker home. In folklore, the shell was considered highly sacred. The two layers are thought to represent the physical and spiritual realms, and the concept of bringing both worlds together.

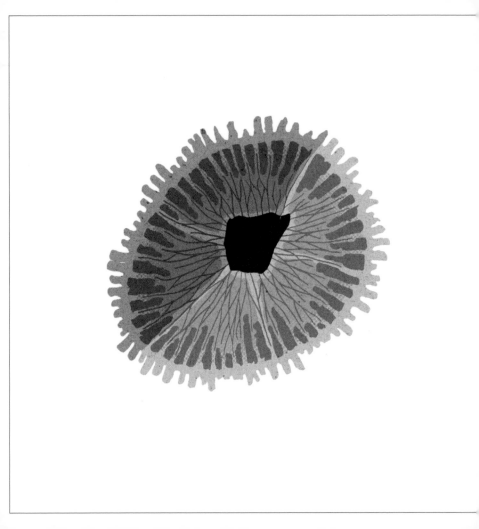

Red Thatch Barnacle

Semibalanus cariosus

FAMILY NAME Balanidae

DESCRIPTION This barnacle has a coarse outer wall, with ribbing that looks like a thatched roof; the plates that form the outer wall can be white, grey, green or brown

SIZE Grows up to 5 cm (2 in) tall and 6 cm (2⅜ in) in diameter

HABITAT Attached to rocks, floats and pilings on exposed shorelines

DISTRIBUTION Native to the northern Pacific Ocean including Japan, and the Pacific northwest coast of North America; also found from Baja California up to shores near San Francisco

The distinctive ridges that give this barnacle its name are usually more visible in the young, or those living in less crowded habitats. In large groups with limited space the barnacle grows taller, but given a little room to breathe it forms the shape of a volcano, which is why it is often referred to as the Volcanic Barnacle. It has a long life span, which ranges up to 15 years.

Spotter's Guide

This checklist will help you categorise your finds. Whether you're into crustaceans, seaweed or shells, it will give you the basics you need to record your discoveries. A bucket is a useful addition to your beachcombing toolkit, especially if you enjoy rock pooling, or want to sift through items on the shore, but be sure to gently restore creatures to their original hiding place when you're done.

☐ **Velvet Swimming Crab**

Necora puber (p8)

☐ **Royal Starfish**

Astropecten articulatus (p11)

☐ **Tidepool Sculpin**

Oligocottus maculosus (p12)

☐ **Common Nutmeg**

Cancellaria reticulata (p15)

☐ **Hermit Crab**
Paguroidea (p16)

☐ **Common Sea Urchin**
Echinus esculentus (p19)

☐ **Conch Shells**
(p20)

☐ **Black Tegula**
Tegula funebralis (p23)

☐ **Gooseneck Barnacle**
Pollicipes polymerus (p24)

☐ **Mermaid's Purse**
(p27)

☐ **Whelk Shells**

(p28)

☐ **Serrated Wrack**

Fucus serratus (p31)

☐ **Common Mussel**

Mytilus edulis (p32)

☐ **Woolly Sculpin**

Clinocottus analis (p35)

☐ **Common Limpet**

Patella vulgata (p36)

☐ **Quartz Veins**

(p39)

□ **Baltic Tellin**
Limecola balthica (p40)

□ **Shore Crab**
Carcinus maenas (p43)

□ **Irish Moss or Carrageen**
Chondrus crispus (p44)

□ **Hag Stones**
(p47)

□ **Cowrie Shells**
Cypraea (p48)

□ **Dog Whelk**
Nucella lapillus (p51)

☐ **Bladderwrack**

Fucus vesiculosus (p52)

☐ **Common Cockle**

Cerastoderma edule (p55)

☐ **Blood Star**

Henricia leviuscula (p56)

☐ **Granite Pebbles**

(p59)

☐ **Sea Lettuce**

Ulva lactuca (p60)

☐ **Common Starfish**

Asterias rubens (p63)

☐ **Auger Shell**

Turritellinella tricarinata (p64)

☐ **Oarweed**

Laminaria digitata (p67)

☐ **Mediterranean Green Crab**

Carcinus aestuarii (p68)

☐ **Sea Glass**

(p71)

☐ **Sand Dollars**

Dendraster excentricus (p72)

☐ **Common Goby**

Pomatoschistus microps (p75)

☐ **Purple Shore Crab**

Hemigrapsus nudus (p76)

☐ **Beadlet Anemone**

Actinia equina (p79)

☐ **Pink Sea Star**

Pisaster brevispinus (p80)

☐ **Sea Hare**

Aplysia punctata (p83)

☐ **Scallop Shells**

(p84)

☐ **Red Thatch Barnacle**

Semibalanus cariosus (p87)

TOM FROST
Print Maker

Print maker and illustrator Tom Frost graduated from
Falmouth College of Arts in 2001, returning to his home
town of Bristol to work as an illustrator for a number
of years. He now divides his time between printmaking,
restoring his crumbling Georgian house in rural Wales
and raising a young family. In recent years he has worked
with clients including the V&A, Perry's Cider, Art Angels,
Freight Household Goods, *Selvedge* magazine, Betty &
Dupree, The Archivist and Yorkshire Sculpture Park. His
work highlights a fascination for old matchboxes, stamps,
folk art, tin toys, children's books and the natural world.

MANAGING DIRECTOR Sarah Lavelle
SENIOR COMMISSIONING EDITOR
Harriet Butt
ASSISTANT EDITOR Oreolu Grillo
SERIES DESIGNER Emily Lapworth
DESIGNER Alicia House
ILLUSTRATOR Tom Frost
WORDS Alison Davies
SENIOR PRODUCTION CONTROLLER
Sabeena Atchia

Published in 2023 by Quadrille, an imprint
of Hardie Grant Publishing

Quadrille
52–54 Southwark Street
London SE1 1UN
quadrille.com

Cataloguing in Publication Data:
a catalogue record for this book is
available from the British Library.

ISBN 978 1 78713 959 6
Printed in China using soy inks